Holt Literature &

Introductory

MW01240973

At Home
A Guide to Standards Mastery
English-Language Edition

for
Holt Literature & Language Arts
Holt Handbook

HOLT, RINEHART AND WINSTON

A Harcourt Classroom Education Company

Austin · New York · Orlando · Atlanta · San Francisco · Boston · Dallas · Toronto · London

STAFF CREDITS

EDITORIAL

Manager, Operations and Planning
Bill Wahlgren

Executive Editors
Robert R. Hoyt, Katie Vignery

Project Editor
David Bradford

Component Editors
Randy Dickson, Amy Fleming

Writing and Editing
Thomas Browne, Gail Coupland, Amber Rigney

Copyediting
Michael Neibergall, *Copyediting Manager;* Mary Malone, *Copyediting Supervisor;* Christine Altgelt, Joel Bourgeois, Elizabeth Dickson, Emily Force, Julie A. Hill, Julia Thomas Hu, Jennifer Kirkland, Millicent Ondras, Dennis Scharnberg, *Copyeditors*

Project Administration
Marie Price, *Managing Editor;* Lori De La Garza, *Editorial Operations Coordinator;* Heather Cheyne, Mark Holland, Marcus Johnson, Jennifer Renteria, Janet Riley, Kelly Tankersley, *Project Administration;* Ruth Hooker, Joie Pickett, Margaret Sanchez, *Word Processing*

Editorial Permissions
Janet Harrington, *Permissions Editor*

ART, DESIGN AND PHOTO

Graphic Services
Eric Rupprath, *Designer*

Image Acquisitions
Joe London, *Director;* Jeannie Taylor, *Photo Research Supervisor,* Tim Taylor, *Photo Research Supervisor;* Rick Benavides, *Photo Researcher;* Cindy Verheyden, *Senior Photo Researcher,* Elaine Tate, *Supervisor*

Cover Design
Curtis Riker, *Director*
Sunday Patterson, *Designer*

PRODUCTION/ MANUFACTURING
Belinda Barbosa Lopez, *Senior Production Coordinator*
Carol Trammel, *Production Supervisor*
Beth Prevelige, *Senior Production Manager*

Printed in the United States of America

ISBN 0-03-066353-9

1 2 3 4 5 022 03 02 01

Table of Contents

Section One

Section Two

Section Three

To the Teacher

At Home: A Guide to Standards Mastery is a selection of letters written for the parents or guardians of students using *Holt Literature and Language Arts* and the *Holt Handbook*. Each letter suggests activities that can be completed at home to extend the material in these textbooks. The activities also help students meet the requirements set forth in the *English–Language Arts Content Standards for California Public Schools*.

Presented in clear and simple language, each letter suggests an activity that the parent or guardian can do with the student. By doing these activities, the parent or guardian participates in the student's education and helps foster an atmosphere in the home that encourages academic success. The letters do not have to be returned to you, do not require a grade, and do not assume that the parent or guardian will read material in the textbooks.

The letters can be used to supplement a chapter or workshop, or they can serve as an independent tool for extending classroom instruction. If a letter has been provided for a particular chapter in *Holt Literature and Language Arts* or the *Holt Handbook*, the Resources box at the beginning of that chapter in the teacher's edition will include a reference to this ancillary.

Section One

This section supports Chapters 1–8 in *Holt Literature and Language Arts*. It contains ten one-page letters, most of which suggest ways a parent or guardian can help a student master the basic requirements of school—for example, completing homework or preparing for tests. Some letters also suggest ways a parent or guardian can help stimulate a student's interest in reading.

Section Two

This section supports Workshops 1–5 in *Holt Literature and Language Arts*. It contains five two-page letters that suggest ways a parent or guardian can help a student complete different writing and speaking assignments.

Section Three

This section supports Chapters 1–16 in the *Holt Handbook*. It contains ten one-page letters; using everyday examples, each letter clarifies a selected topic relating to grammar, usage, and mechanics.

Section One

Getting Your Child Organized

Dear Parent or Guardian,

As your child grows academically, so does his or her workload. In addition to mastering the California Reading Standards, your child will be learning skills in all school subjects and juggling several homework assignments. You can use the following tips to help your child stay organized.

COLOR CODE FOR SUCCESS Your child will be studying many different subjects in school this year. At the end of the school day, while rushing to leave, your child may accidentally leave behind materials needed at home. To help your child quickly identify needed materials, provide him or her with different colored notebooks for each subject area.

Also, encourage your child to keep a small notebook handy during the school day. In it, he or she can jot down reminders of what materials need to be taken home each day.

ORGANIZE A STUDY CENTER Help your child set up a study center in a quiet place. Keep the study center stocked with supplies so that your child won't waste time looking for things.

The study center should also have an area to store frequently used books. Put up a bookshelf to hold your child's textbooks as well as a dictionary and other useful reference books.

Note: If you have a computer with access to the Internet, your child will be able to use electronic versions of dictionaries, thesauruses, and atlases.

Study Center Checklist

Set up the study center in a well-lighted area that is as far from distractions as possible. If it is not possible to put the study center in a separate room, set it off in a corner, and switch off the television and radio while your child is studying.

Supplies	Reference Materials
_____ pens	_____ textbooks
_____ pencils	_____ dictionary
_____ paper (lined)	_____ thesaurus
_____ paper (unlined)	_____ almanac
_____ index cards	_____ atlas
_____ sticky notes	
_____ paper clips or stapler	**Other Materials**
_____ tape	_____ calendar
_____ highlighter	_____ pencil sharpener
	_____ folders

Improving Your Child's Study Skills

Dear Parent or Guardian,

Throughout the year, your child will be studying various subject areas. Strong study skills will help your child master the California Reading Standards as well as standards in other subjects. You can use the following suggestions to help your child's study skills improve.

SET A TIME AND PLACE Setting a routine may help improve your child's study skills. Work with your child to decide on a time of day to set aside for schoolwork, and then have your child stick to the schedule as closely as possible. Don't allow your child to "study" while listening to music or in front of the television. Save those activities for when the homework is complete.

SET STUDY GOALS Help your child complete the Study Goals Worksheet below. Encourage your child to record questions that remain after studying to bring up with the teacher.

Study Tips for Your Child

- Work in a quiet place.
- Gather all needed materials before starting the assignment.
- When work is finished, pack up book bag for the next day.

Study Goals Worksheet			
Assignment/ When Due	**How Much Time Will It Take?**	**What I Need to Complete the Assignment**	**Questions for Teacher**

Talking with the Teacher

Dear Parent or Guardian,

Parent/teacher conferences help you learn how well your child is mastering the California Reading Standards. A little preparation can help you make the most of these valuable discussions. Use the following tips.

BEFORE THE CONFERENCE Prepare for the conference by having an interview (below) with your child. Listen to your child's responses, and take notes. Write down questions you want to ask at the conference.

DURING THE CONFERENCE Bring your notes and questions to the conference. If the teacher's observations don't agree with yours, discuss your different impressions.

You should also talk about your child's behavior and classroom citizenship. Ask the teacher for specific goals your child should reach within the next few semester. Discuss ways you can help.

AFTER THE CONFERENCE Talk with your child about his or her progress. Focus on areas that need improvement, and set goals you can work on together.

Pre-Conference Interview With Your Child

▶ What is your favorite subject? What subject don't you like? Why?

_____

▶ What is the best thing that has happened at school lately? Explain.

_____

▶ What subject is hardest for you?

_____

▶ Is there anything you would like me to talk about with your teacher?

_____

Issues to Bring Up with Teacher	**Goals for My Child**

Improving Your Child's Spelling: Frequently Misspelled Words

Dear Parent or Guardian,

The California Reading Standards encourage the development of consistent spelling. California Written and Oral English-Language Conventions Standard 1.5, in particular, focuses on correcting spelling mistakes that students often make. You can use the following tips to help your child learn correct spellings of tricky words.

RECORD MISSPELLED WORDS Whenever your child misspells a word, write the word (correctly spelled) on the chart below.

Write the word in the first column if your child confused the spellings of two different words. Put other misspelled words in the second column. Post this list on your refrigerator for your child to refer to.

HOME SPELLING Challenge your child to spell words that you find in newspapers, magazines, and advertisements. Use each word in a sentence and ask your child to spell the word. If your child misspells the word, add it to the list below. Practice spelling each word until your child masters it.

Spelling List

Post this chart on your refrigerator, the bathroom mirror, or some other place your child sees often. Add to the chart weekly or as necessary. Every month or so, quiz your child on the words to make sure that he or she remembers how to spell them.

Words Often Confused			Words with Tricky Spellings		
their	there	they're	enough	beautiful	ocean
too	to	two	through	because	friend
its	it's		probably	receive	license

Reinforcing Reading Comprehension: Use Features to Find Information

Dear Parent or Guardian,

Reference sources have many useful features that can help your child find needed information. California Reading Standard 2.1 requires students to use features such as a table of contents, chapter headings, or an index to locate information. You can use the following activity to help your child become comfortable using these features.

Reference Hunt

Post this chart in your kitchen or in your child's study center. Have your child fill out this chart using reference materials available in your home. Whenever a new magazine, book, or newspaper shows up in your home, encourage your child to locate and review each of these features.

Title of Book/ Magazine/Textbook	What the Table of Contents Reveals	What the Chapter or Article Headings Tell Me	What Information Is Found in the Index

Discussing Books with Your Child: Setting and Character

Dear Parent or Guardian,

   To master California Reading Standard 3.3, your child needs to understand story characters and settings. You can help your child master this standard by discussing the stories he or she reads. Take time to talk about any book your child is reading. Ask the following questions, and have your child fill out the following chart with responses.

Character Questions

Use these questions to help your child analyze story characters:

1. What three words would you use to describe the main character?

2. Who does this character remind you of?

3. What is the character's main goal or wish?

4. Does this character change during the story? In what ways?

Setting Questions

Use these questions to help your child analyze story setting:

1. Where does this story take place?

2. When does this story take place?

3. Does the story setting affect the characters in any way? If so, describe how.

4. Would this story be different if it were set someplace else? Why or why not?

Character and Setting Chart

As you discuss stories and books with your child, have your child fill out this chart.

Book Title and Author	
Character Name	**Story Setting(s)**
1.	**1.**
2.	**2.**
3.	**3.**
4.	**4.**

Reinforcing Literary Concepts: Figurative Language

Dear Parent or Guardian,

California Reading Standard 3.4 requires students to read and interpret literary works such as poetry. One of the most important ways poetry communicates is through figurative language—language that isn't meant to be taken literally. You can use the following activities to help your child recognize and use figurative language at home.

TALK FIGURATIVELY You probably use figurative language often at home. For example, you may say that someone is *as strong as an ox* or that something is *as light as a feather*. Along with your child, come up with at least two figurative expressions each day for a week. Add your family's favorites to the chart below.

EARS LIKE DETECTIVES Post the chart, and encourage your child to keep alert for figurative language that occurs in daily speech, in newspapers, and on television. At the end of the week, count the entries with your child and vote for what you think are the most creative and fun entries.

Similes and Metaphors Chart

Read the following examples with your child. Identify the things being compared. Then, help your child come up with several more examples for each list.

A **simile** is a comparison of unlike things that uses *like* or *as*.	A **metaphor** is a comparison of unlike things that does not use *like* or *as*.
Examples:	Examples:
• Her smile was as bright as a neon sign. (*Smile* is being compared to *neon sign*.)	• The sun is a bright gold coin. (*Sun* is compared to *gold coin*.)
• My little brother stuck to me like glue. (*Little brother* is being compared to *glue*.)	• The stars are diamonds in the sky. (*Stars* are compared to *diamonds*.)
•	•
•	•
•	•
•	•

Practicing Fluency with Your Child: Reading Aloud

Dear Parent or Guardian,

The ability to read aloud with ease and confidence is a part of your child's development emphasized in California's educational framework. You can help your child perfect this skill by making reading aloud a part of daily family life. The following suggestions will help strengthen your child's reading skills.

AFTER-DINNER READING Develop a family reading habit. After dinner, for example, a family member could read a story, article, or poem aloud while the others clean up. Be sure to switch the reading role frequently—have a new reader every five or ten minutes, or pick a new reader each night.

REREAD FAVORITES Keep a list of the readings that your child enjoys most. Once a week, encourage your child to pick one of these items and re-read it. You will probably notice a strong improvement each time your child reads the same item—practice makes perfect!

Tips for Reading Aloud

Share these tips with your child to improve his or her reading ability:

- **Read slowly.** Listeners need time to hear each word.

- **Use punctuation.** Pause briefly at commas, and come to a full stop at periods.

- **Speak up.** Your audience wants to hear what you're reading.

- **Find variety.** Once you are familiar with a reading, try to find ways to change your tone of voice, reading speed, and word emphasis. Variety will make your reading more interesting and effective.

Favorite Readings

From time to time, have your child add favorite books to this list. Once a week, have your child choose a work from this list to read aloud from.

Book Title
1.
2.
3.
4.
5.

AT HOME: A GUIDE TO STANDARDS MASTERY | Introductory Course

Expanding Your Child's Vocabulary: Words with Multiple Meanings

Dear Parent or Guardian,

California Reading Standard 1.2 calls for students to identify and interpret words with multiple meanings. You can use the following activities to help your child recognize and use words with multiple meanings.

DOUBLE MEANINGS Point out to your child that many words have more than one meaning. Read these two sentences with your child:

- The *general* idea is clear, but the details are not.
- The soldiers took orders from the *general*.

Although spelled the same in each sentence, *general* is used in completely different ways.

WORD WATCH Post the chart below, and use it to collect examples of multiple-meaning words you and your child find in newspapers, magazines, books, and other reading materials. Each time your child adds a word, check that the spelling and definitions are correct. Every now and again, review the words in the chart by using them in sentences. Each time, ask your child which definition of the word you are using.

Words with More than One Meaning	
general	_____
1. not specific, relating to the whole	**1.**
2. high-ranking military officer	**2.**
_____	_____
1.	**1.**
2.	**2.**
_____	_____
1.	**1.**
2.	**2.**
_____	_____
1.	**1.**
2.	**2.**

Keeping the Summer Productive: Encouraging Independent Reading

Dear Parent or Guardian,

The California instructional framework emphasizes the importance of independent reading in your child's life. Summer vacation offers a great opportunity for your child to read independently and develop a love of learning. You can use the following suggestions to help your child create a fun and inspiring summer reading schedule.

SET GOALS Help your child set specific summer reading goals. Reading a variety of books will help expand your child's interests and knowledge. Suggest that your child plan to read at least one book in each category below. Encourage your child to talk with the local librarian for specific reading ideas.

CHART PROGRESS Keep track of your child's reading by posting this page and drawing a star for each finished book. Highlight an entire row when your child reaches the goal for a specific genre or book type. When your child finishes all of his or her summer reading goals, provide an appropriate—and enthusiastic—reward.

Summer Reading Goals		
	Goal	**Books Read**
FICTION		
Short Stories		
Novels		
Poetry		
NONFICTION		
Science		
History		
Biography/Autobiography		

Section Two

Listening and Speaking: How to Be a Good Listener

Dear Parent or Guardian,

In the Listening and Speaking Workshops found in the Writing Workshop sections of *Holt Literature and Language Arts*, your child learns how to deliver and evaluate oral reports. This letter lets you know what is expected of your child in these workshops. It also gives you some suggestions to help your child master the California Listening and Speaking Standards.

Holt Literature and Language Arts gives your sixth-grader many ways to master listening and speaking techniques:

- In Listening and Speaking Workshop 1, students learn how to deliver an oral narrative, and listen to and evaluate their classmates' narratives.
- In Listening and Speaking Workshop 2, students learn how to listen for information or instructions, and take notes that will allow them to restate the information.
- In Listening and Speaking Workshop 3, students learn how to adapt the short story they wrote in Writing Workshop 1 into an oral presentation. They also learn how to listen to and evaluate their classmates' stories.
- In Listening and Speaking Workshop 4, students learn how to adapt and deliver their research report, and listen to and evaluate their classmates' narratives.
- In Listening and Speaking Workshop 5, students learn how to deliver a convincing persuasive speech, and listen to and evaluate their classmates' persuasive speeches.

The Importance of Listening

The ability to listen is important in school, and it will be just as important when your child becomes an adult. Your child's teachers expect him or her to listen well, even as the teaching material gets more complex and homework is given more often. Missing a test date, a homework due date, or an important point in class will obviously hurt your child's chances for success, just as not following your boss's directions at work isn't the best way to get a promotion!

Luckily, listening skills are easy to learn and remember. The following list can help improve listening skills. You might want to go through the list with your child.

- Look at the speaker, and pay attention.
- Do not interrupt the speaker. Do not whisper, fidget, or make distracting noises or movements.
- Respect the speaker's race, accent, clothing, customs, and religion.
- Try to understand the speaker's point of view. Remember that your own point of view or attitude toward the topic affects your judgment.
- Listen to the entire message before you form an opinion about it.
- Take notes. Do not write down every word. Instead, focus on the most important details.

Activities

To help your child practice listening skills, you might want to do either or both of the following activities with him or her.

1. Look in a TV schedule with your child for a home-improvement show, a cooking show, or something similar. These kinds of shows tell their viewers how to complete a specific task. For example, a cooking show might give the viewers a recipe for oatmeal cookies. Ask your child to watch the show and write down the steps of the process. Tell him or her to keep the following things in mind:

   • Pay attention to transitional words, words that indicate the order of the steps in the process. *First, second, next, then,* and *finally* are all examples of transitional words.

   EXAMPLE First, grease the pan. **Then,** pour the batter in the pan.

   • Pay attention to spatial words, words that indicate where things should be placed.

   EXAMPLE Next, place the dough **on the pan.** Place the pan **in the oven.**

   • Don't try to remember every word, but try to pick out all of the important steps.

2. Some TV shows rely on effective and clear speaking skills to attract and maintain large audiences. To give your child some practice evaluating the skill of a speaker, ask your child to listen to two different speakers on TV and compare them. A good comparison might be made between the anchor, or speaker, on the local evening news and the anchor on a national news program. Your child might want to watch an interview show and compare the speaking skills of the guest and the host. Whatever speakers your child compares, tell him or her to keep the following things in mind.

   • Pay attention to the tempo, or speed, of the speaker's voice. Is the speaker easy to understand, or are the words too fast or slow?

   • Pay attention to the body language of the speaker. Body language is the way the speaker moves while he or she is speaking. Good body language should reinforce the speaker's words and not distract the audience.

You might want to use the following chart as a guide.

Category	Speaker One	Speaker Two
Tempo		
Body Language		
General		

Helping Your Child Develop an Idea for a Short Story

Dear Parent or Guardian,

In Workshop 1 of *Holt Literature and Language Arts*, students learn how to write a *short story* (California Writing Standard 2.1). A short story has a simple plot and only a few characters. Using the activities in this letter, you can help your sixth-grader develop ideas for short stories.

Steps for Developing Short-Story Ideas

Most homework assignments ask students to show that they understand what the teacher has already taught them. For example, a math teacher might show students how to work a certain kind of problem in class, and then assign the same kind of problem as homework so that students can show that they understand what was taught. Writing a short story is a little different; students have to use imagination to come up with story ideas. Most students learn to enjoy this freedom, but they might need some help getting started. The following list suggests how you can help your child come up with some good story ideas.

1. Have your child begin by thinking about interesting people and the kinds of problems that they might face. These characters may be made up or based on real people. For example, the people your child sees on the TV news, hears about in stories told by family members, or meets in the real world might make good characters for a short story.

2. Next, have your child choose a problem that the character will face. As in real life, problems give short stories drama, interest, and action. Sometimes an interesting problem can be the inspiration for a short story.

3. Show your child the two-column chart below, which contains possible characters and problems for a short story. By mixing and matching the characters and problems in this chart and adding some details, your child might be able to come up with some interesting story ideas.

Possible Characters	Possible Problems
• a young camper	• a big storm
• a hungry cat	• a talking bird
• an ashamed thief	• a stolen bicycle
• a very large clown	• a flat tire
• a clever sixth-grade student	• a missing aunt
• a kindhearted janitor	• a runaway school bus
• an eccentric neighbor	• a newly discovered treasure map
• a juggler on the street	• an overturned fruit cart

4. Next, have your child write out a story idea in a few sentences. He or she can use the following example as a model.

EXAMPLE In my short story a young camper, named Bob, faces a problem. The problem is that he is caught in a big storm while he and his family are on vacation.

This writer chose a character, "a young camper," and a problem, "a big storm," from the list. Notice how the writer added additional details to complete the idea.

5. Have your child choose a character and a problem from the chart. Ask him or her to complete the following sentences with the appropriate information.

In my short story, *(choose a character from the chart:)* _____

named_____ faces a problem. The problem is that *(choose a problem from the chart, and*

add a few more details to complete the idea:) _____

_____

_____

_____.

Alternate Activity

Using the chart in step three as a model, help your child come up with original characters and problems. On separate sheets of paper, one of you could write down eight characters while the other makes up eight problems that a character might have to face. Then, each of you could copy your list into the chart below. To make it more interesting, choose the most unusual and outlandish ideas you can think of. Work together to see if you can get a few good ideas for short stories.

Possible Characters	Possible Problems
•	•
•	•
•	•
•	•
•	•
•	•
•	•
•	•

How to Write a "How-to" Essay

Dear Parent or Guardian,

    In Workshop 2 of *Holt Literature and Language Arts*, students learn how to write a *"how-to" essay* (California Writing Standard 2.2). The purpose of a "how-to" essay is to tell someone how to do something. In a "how-to" essay, a writer uses specific details and *transitional words*—words that connect one idea to another—to give exact instructions for making a product. This letter gives you an activity that you can do with your sixth-grader to help choose a topic for a "how-to" essay and make an outline for it.

Activity

1. The first step in writing a "how-to" essay is to choose a topic. Your child should follow the rule of many successful writers: *Write about what you know.* Have your child make a list of products that he or she has made before. Ask your child to consider the following questions:

   - Look around your home. Do you see anything that you built or made?
   - What school projects have you made in the past?
   - What is your favorite recipe to make?

   Using these activities, ask your child to choose three products that he or she has made.

2. Once your child has listed three products, he or she will need to evaluate them to choose the best one to write about. The following chart shows how one child decided on one of three topics by asking questions about each topic. Read through the example chart with your child.

EXAMPLE

Topic	Have I made this product before, and do I know the process well?	Does this process have a manageable number of steps (between three and five)?
Paper swan	yes	no—it has over five steps
Snowman decoration	yes	yes—it has about five steps
Soapbox car	not really—I helped my big brother make it	no—it probably has more than five steps

Based upon the answers to the two questions, this student chose to write a "how-to" essay on the snowman decoration. The student has made the product before, and the process involves between three and five steps.

Now, have your child use the chart below to evaluate the three ideas that he or she chose. Have your child choose the best of the three topics.

Activity

Topic	Have I made this product before, and do I know the process well?	Does this process have a manageable number of steps (between three and five)?

3. Finally, ask your child to complete the following sentences by filling in the steps of the process. Filling in these steps can help your child organize the elements of his or her essay. The first sentence asks your child to fill in the name of the product. The next sentences, introduced by transitional words, ask for brief descriptions of each important step. (If your child's process requires only three or four steps, have him or her skip one or two of the middle sentences and go to the last sentence.)

In my "how-to" essay I will explain how to _____

_____ .

First, _____

_____ .

Then, _____

_____ .

Next, _____

_____ .

Next, _____

_____ .

Finally, _____

_____ .

Your child now has an outline of a "how-to" essay. By adding more details and more complete descriptions of each step in the process, your child will be able to turn this outline into a well-organized essay.

Helping Your Child Write a Research Report

Dear Parent or Guardian,

In Workshop 4 of *Holt Literature and Language Arts*, students learn how to write a *research report* (California Writing Standard 2.3). In a research report, a writer gathers information on a topic from different sources and then shares the information with others. This letter gives you an activity that you can do with your sixth-grader to help with the first step in writing a research report: finding an interesting and manageable subject.

Finding a Subject for a Research Report

1. Here are some ways that your child can use to find possible subjects for a research report.

   • Make an "I wonder" log (*I wonder why cats purr . . ., how helicopters fly . . ., who discovered electricity . . .*).

   • Browse a television guide, magazine, or newspaper for interesting subjects (people in the news, medical marvels, strange animals, space technology . . .).

2. Once your child has a list of possible subjects, he or she can choose the most interesting one. Your child will need to focus on a part of the subject that is small enough to be covered in one report. For example, suppose he or she is interested in animals. If your child tried to write a research report about "animals," the amount of research needed to cover everything, from fleas to whales, would be overwhelming. Therefore, to make the task easier your child should narrow the subject down to a focused topic. Here is an example of one way to focus a subject.

EXAMPLE

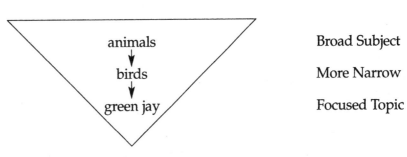

3. Now, ask your child to use the following chart to focus his or her subject.

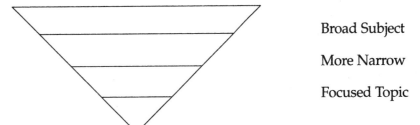

4. At this point, your child could begin doing research on his or her topic. However, one final step, called a clustering exercise, might be helpful. Clustering is a way for writers to map out their ideas before writing. Creating a visual outline of the information can help your child discover how much he or she knows about the subject and which parts are the most interesting. Have your child do the following:

• Write the topic in the center of a sheet of paper and draw a circle around it.

• Think of some specific elements, or subtopics, of that topic. Write them around the main topic, draw circles around them, and connect each new (subtopic) circle to the first (topic) circle with a line.

• Add any important details or elements of each subtopic, draw circles around them, and connect them with lines to the subtopic circle.

Here's how the example from step two might look.

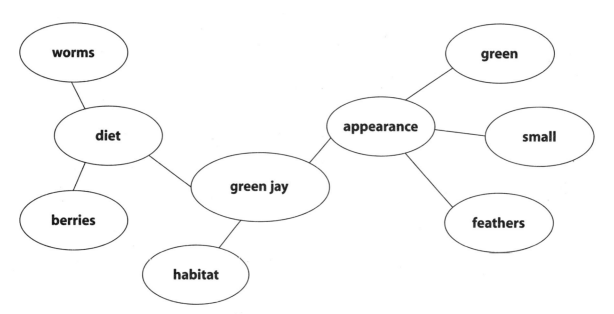

Helping Your Child Recognize Propaganda on TV

Dear Parent or Guardian,

In Workshop 5 of *Holt Literature and Language Arts*, students learn how to identify propaganda techniques on TV (California Listening and Speaking Strategy 1.9). Using suggestions in this letter, you can help your child identify propaganda techniques that are commonly used on TV.

Propaganda is a method of persuasion that appeals to emotions more than to common sense or logic. Some of the most common propaganda techniques—the ones you probably see every day, sometimes without realizing it—appear in TV commercials and, occasionally, on TV shows. A group of people who sing and dance after sipping a soft drink, a cuddly animal holding a tissue, a medicine recommended by "four out of five doctors"—each is an example of propaganda.

A TV commercial's job is to get you to buy the product in the commercial. Although there are laws to keep a commercial from lying outright, it may bend the truth a little. Propaganda techniques try to make a product look its very best, at the same time hiding what might be wrong with it. By accepting at face value messages that contain propaganda techniques, a viewer may make poor decisions. Knowing those techniques can help your child become a more careful and informed viewer.

How to Spot Propaganda Techniques on TV

If you're like most people, you watch television for the shows and not for the commercials. However, this activity works the other way around. You and your child will watch the commercials to find propaganda techniques, using the following steps as a guide. Some propaganda techniques may appear in the show itself.

1. Before you begin watching, read through the chart on the next page. It contains some of the most common propaganda techniques. A short definition of each technique is given, followed by a clue for detecting the propaganda and an example of how it might look on TV.

2. Pick a show to watch together. Keep in mind that commercials are made to appeal to the audience watching the show. For example, your child's favorite after-school show isn't likely to have car commercials, just as your favorite prime-time drama probably won't have ads for the latest toy. For this activity, you'll probably want to watch a show written for a younger audience.

3. On a separate sheet of paper, have your child list the commercials as they come on, then try to identify the propaganda technique being used. Don't worry if the commercial ends too quickly or a technique isn't obvious at first; most commercials come on more than once during a show, so there's no rush.

Propaganda Techniques Used on Television

Techniques	Clues	Examples
Bandwagon tries to convince you to do something or believe something because everyone else does.	Listen for slogans that use the words *everyone, everybody, all,* or in some cases, *nobody.*	A person wearing a particular brand of clothing is so happy, she starts dancing down the sidewalk. By the end of the commercial, everybody else on the sidewalk is dancing with her.
Loaded language uses words with strongly positive or negative meanings.	Listen for strongly positive or negative words, such as *perfect* or *terrible.*	*Wake-up Juice is the perfect way to start your day!*
Product placement uses brand-name products as part of a show's scenery. The products' companies may pay producers for this seemingly accidental advertising.	As you watch the show, keep your eyes peeled for clearly visible brand names. Ask yourself if the brand names have anything to do with the plot of the show.	In the middle of a show, an actor may drink a bottle of juice. The juice is not an important part of the story, but the brand name of the juice is clearly visible.
Snob appeal suggests that a viewer can be extra special or part of a special group if he or she agrees with an idea or buys a product.	Listen for words such as *exclusive, best,* or *quality.* Look for images of wealth, such as big houses, expensive cars, and fancy boats.	*Treat your cat like a queen; give her the cat food preferred exclusively by discriminating cats.*
Symbols associate the power and meaning of a cultural symbol with a product or idea.	Look for flags, team mascots, state flowers, or any other symbol that people view with pride.	A political candidate might use a national flag as a backdrop for a speech on TV.

Section Three

Identifying Simple and Compound Sentences

Dear Parent or Guardian,

Your child's class is now using Chapter 4 of the *Holt Handbook* to learn about simple and compound sentences (California Written and Oral English-Language Conventions Standard 1.1). To give your child more practice with these two kinds of sentences, you may wish to use the following activity.

A *simple sentence* expresses a complete thought that can stand on its own.

> **SIMPLE SENTENCE** I like music.

NOT A SIMPLE SENTENCE When he left.

A *compound sentence* is made up of two or more simple sentences usually joined by a comma and the conjunction *and*, *but*, *for*, *nor*, *or*, *so*, or *yet*.

> **COMPOUND SENTENCE** Sondra liked the skit**, but** Katy thought it was silly.

NOT A COMPOUND SENTENCE He picked a flower **and** gave it to his mother for her birthday.

Compound or Not Compound?

STEP 1 Find a magazine or newspaper article. Then, together with your child, scan the article and underline sentences that contain the conjunctions *and*, *but*, *for*, *nor*, *or*, *so*, or *yet*.

> **EXAMPLES** She stood up **and** discussed the three major points of her proposal.
> Kelly hit the ball to an outfielder, **but** he dropped it.

STEP 2 Now, ask your child to identify any of the underlined sentences that are compound. To help your child, have him or her put a finger over each conjunction and tell whether the words on each side of his or her finger can stand on their own as a simple sentence. If so, the sentence is probably compound.

> **EXAMPLES** She stood up **and** discussed the three major points of her proposal. ["She stood up" can stand on its own; "discussed the three major points of her proposal" can't. The sentence is not compound.]
> Kelly hit the ball to an outfielder, **but** he dropped it. ["Kelly hit the ball to an outfielder" can stand on its own; "he dropped it" can, too. The sentence is compound.]

STEP 3 To extend the activity, you may want to help your child complete Steps 1 and 2 of this activity with one of his or her completed writing assignments. If the assignment has no compound sentences, encourage your child to create a couple. After all, using different kinds of sentences can help your child create a lively style.

Using Verbs That Agree with Compound Subjects

Dear Parent or Guardian,

Your sixth-grader is studying Chapter 6 of the *Holt Handbook* to learn about using verbs with compound subjects (California Written and Oral English-Language Conventions Standard 1.2). To give your child practice with this skill, you may wish to use the following information.

A *compound subject* is made up of two or more subjects usually connected by *and* or *or*. A compound subject connected by *and* usually needs a plural verb.

EXAMPLE The **student and the instructor of the class were practicing** for the tournament. [Both the student and the instructor were practicing.]

When a compound subject is connected by *or*, the verb needs to agree with the subject that is closer to the verb.

EXAMPLES The students or **the instructor of the class demonstrates** new moves. [Either the students *or* the instructor is demonstrating. Because the subject *instructor* is closer to the verb, the verb agrees with *instructor*.]

The instructor of the class or **the students demonstrate** new moves. [Either the instructor *or* the students are demonstrating. Because the subject *students* is closer to the verb, the verb agrees with *students*.]

Describing Your Favorite Band

STEP 1 Have your child imagine that a local radio station is sponsoring a contest called "Bands and Their Fans." The winner of the contest gets to spend a day with his or her favorite band. To enter, each contestant must submit a brief paragraph about his or her favorite band. Ask your child to take notes for the paragraph by completing the following sentences. All of the sentences have compound subjects.

    1. My favorite band's music and appearance _____.

    2. Neither the lead singer nor the musicians _____.

    3. On their latest CD, the first song and the last song _____.

    4. A poster or a T-shirt _____.

STEP 2 Now, ask your child to add more sentences to his or her notes. This time, the sentences can be more specific, including such information as the band's name, names of the members, and titles of songs. Encourage the use of as many compound subjects as possible.

    EXAMPLE His unusual guitar solos and funny lyrics make every song sound different.

STEP 3 If you wish, have your child continue the activity by writing the paragraph as if it were to be submitted to the radio station's contest. You may also decide to have some fun by talking about your favorite band.

Using Verbs That Agree with Indefinite Pronouns

Dear Parent or Guardian,

   Your sixth-grader is now studying Chapter 6 of the *Holt Handbook* to learn about indefinite pronouns (California Written and Oral English-Language Conventions Standard 1.2). You may wish to use the following activity to give your child practice making indefinite pronouns agree with their verbs.

A *singular indefinite pronoun* needs a singular verb.

Singular Indefinite Pronouns

anybody	anyone	anything	each	one	something
either	everybody	everyone	everything	somebody	
neither	nobody	no one	nothing	someone	

EXAMPLES **Anything is** possible. [The singular verb *is* agrees with the singular pronoun *Anything*.]
Everybody on the team **likes** the coach. [The singular verb *likes* agrees with the singular pronoun *Everybody*.]

Creating an Advertisement

Because indefinite pronouns don't refer to anyone in particular, they are frequently used in advertisements to appeal to the widest possible audience.

STEP 1 Together, make a list of ideas for new products or services. Then, choose the best idea and give a few details about it. If you'd like, you can even take an existing product or service and change it in some way.

  EXAMPLE grocery delivery service—inexpensive, door-to-door delivery of basic groceries to people in our neighborhood

STEP 2 Next, help your sixth-grader come up with one or two general statements that might help the product or service sell. These general statements should include singular indefinite pronouns and singular verbs. Here is an example of a general statement.

  EXAMPLE **Everyone needs** groceries.

STEP 3 Finally, help your child write a brief paragraph—four or five sentences will do—to advertise the product or service. The paragraph should include the general statements that you and your child wrote. Also include any other information necessary to describe the product or service and its benefits.

  EXAMPLE **Everyone needs** groceries. The problem is that **no one seems** to have enough time to go to the store. Well, the people at Neighborhood Grocery Delivery do! For an affordable fee, we'll go to the store, pick up the groceries on your list, and deliver them to your front door …

   If you and your child would like to extend the activity, you might finish the ad by including original artwork or clippings from magazines or newspapers.

Understanding Perfect Tense

Dear Parent or Guardian,

Your sixth-grader is studying verb tenses in Chapter 7 of the *Holt Handbook* (California Written and Oral English-Language Conventions Standard 1.2). You may wish to use the following information to help your child understand the past perfect verb tense.

A verb in the *past tense* describes an event or condition that happened or existed at an unspecified point in the past.

> **PAST**   Jason **read** the story. [Jason read the story sometime in the past.]

Unlike the past tense, a verb in the *past perfect tense* describes an event or condition that happened or existed before a specific time in the past. To form the past perfect tense, put *had* before the verb.

PAST PERFECT   Jason **had read** the story before class began. [The reading of the story took place before a specific time: before class started.]

Been There, Done That

STEP 1   Together with your child, talk about how much your child has accomplished over the years. Then, help your child list several of these accomplishments. Then, identify the approximate age at the time of each accomplishment. Use the chart below as a guide.

Accomplishment	Approximate age
walked for the first time	by the time I was one year old
successfully rode a bicycle without training wheels	before my sixth birthday
sang a solo in the school play	after I turned ten years old

STEP 2   Next, help your child write a sentence for each of the accomplishments listed. Each sentence should use the past perfect tense.

> **EXAMPLES**   By the time I was one year old, **I had learned** to walk.
> I **had ridden** a bicycle without training wheels before I turned six.
> After I **had turned** ten, I sang a solo in the school play.

STEP 3   To extend this activity, you may want to help your child create a scrapbook or an album highlighting his or her accomplishments. Your child could include photographs or decorate the pages with original artwork or clippings from magazines and newspapers.

Using *Their, There,* and *They're*

Dear Parent or Guardian,

In the sixth grade, students are using Chapter 10 of the *Holt Handbook* to learn about words that are commonly misused (California Written and Oral English-Language Conventions Standard 1.5). To provide your child with practice with one set of commonly misused words—*their, there,* and *they're*—you may wish to use the activity provided in this letter.

Although the words **their, there,** and **they're** sound alike, they each have a different meaning.

EXAMPLES Is **their** story believable? [*Their* is used to show ownership.]

Over **there** is your missing sweater. [*There* is used to mean "at that place."]

There are three apples left. [*There* can also be used to begin a sentence.]

They're planning an afternoon picnic. [*They're* is a combination of the words *they* and *are*.]

Creature Feature

STEP 1 Discuss with your sixth-grader the meanings of the words *their, there,* and *they're*, using the examples above. Then, encourage your child to come up with a group of imaginary creatures. Help generate ideas by asking "Where do they live? What color are they? How many arms and legs do they have? Where are their eyes located?" and so on.

STEP 2 Next, help your child write a brief description of the creatures. Use *their, there,* and *they're* correctly at least once in the description.

EXAMPLE **There** are five strange creatures living under my bed. **They're** three inches tall and two inches wide, and they like to squeal and jump. **Their** horns are yellow, **their** feet are blue, and all six arms are green. **Their** tails are long and polka-dotted and **their** belly buttons are, too. I'm not sure how they got **there,** but **they're** perfectly welcome to stay—as long as they let me sleep.

STEP 3 Once your child has finished, have him or her go back through the description and underline or highlight all uses of the words *their, there,* and *they're*. To extend this activity, your child could draw the imaginary creatures or write a story or poem about them.

Capitalizing Proper Nouns

Dear Parent or Guardian,

   Your sixth-grader is studying capitalization (California Written and Oral English-Language Conventions Standard 1.4), which is discussed in Chapter 11 of the *Holt Handbook*. The following activity is designed to help you give your child extra practice capitalizing proper nouns.

Capitalize the names of specific people, places, things, and ideas.

EXAMPLES Jerome Evanson   Orlando, Florida   Grand Canyon   Jupiter
                   Memorial Day   World Trade Center   Pacific Ocean   *Great Expectations*

Local Attractions

STEP 1 What kinds of things make your community special? With your child, list several categories such as the ones below to answer this question. Point out that none of the categories require capitalization because they don't name specific people, places, things, or ideas.

   EXAMPLES favorite restaurant   sports team
                    popular attraction   funny radio personality

STEP 2 Next, go through the categories from Step 1 and list a choice for each category. Have your child do the same on a separate sheet of paper. Be sure to point out that each of the choices in Step 2 should be capitalized because each will name a specific person, place, thing, or idea.

   EXAMPLES favorite restaurant   Three Rivers Cafe
                    sports team   Clearview Panthers

STEP 3 When the lists are complete, have some fun comparing them. Which choices are the same and which are different? To extend this activity, you might encourage your child to use the categories from Step 1 to poll his or her classmates. You might also use the steps in this activity to list things that make other communities or places special.

Capitalizing Geographical Names

Dear Parent or Guardian,

One requirement of students in the sixth grade is to capitalize geographical names correctly (California Written and Oral English-Language Conventions Standard 1.4). Capitalization is discussed in Chapter 11 of the *Holt Handbook*. You may want to use this activity to help your child with capitalization.

Geographical names should be capitalized.

EXAMPLES   Last year, we visited **G**lacier **B**ay **N**ational **P**ark in **A**laska.
Ken's flight to **A**lbuquerque, **N**ew **M**exico, was delayed.

Oh, the Places You'll See!

STEP 1   To give your child practice capitalizing the names of geographical locations, help him or her plan a dream vacation. Ask your child, "If you could go anywhere in the world, where would you go?" You might use an atlas, globe, travel brochures, or magazines to help your child come up with ideas. Would your child plan a trip across the United States, a trip to a theme park, or a trip across Europe?

STEP 2   Next, have your child make a list of five places he or she would like to visit. Encourage him or her to capitalize the names of the places correctly.

EXAMPLES   **M**esa **V**erde **N**ational **P**ark in **C**olorado
Hawaii

Then, have your child write sentences that tell what he or she would like to do at each vacation spot.

EXAMPLES   I want to go hiking in Mesa Verde National Park in Colorado.
I would love to snorkel in the blue waters surrounding Hawaii.

STEP 3   If your child wants to learn more about a vacation spot, he or she might want to do some research. Your child could look up the geographical location on the Internet or order travel brochures through the mail.

Using Semicolons

Dear Parent or Guardian,

Students in the sixth grade are learning about semicolons (California Written and Oral English-Language Conventions Standard 1.3). The use of semicolons to join related sentences is discussed in Chapter 12 of the *Holt Handbook*. You may want to use this activity to provide your child with extra practice using semicolons.

A *semicolon* is used to join two sentences that are closely related in meaning.

EXAMPLE Whenever we go to the park, Simon and Aurora enjoy watching birds; I prefer hiking.

A Few of My Favorite Things

STEP 1 To begin the activity, have your child fill in the left-hand chart below for his or her favorite snack, sport, and so on. Then, do the same for your chart. Try to come up with different responses than those that your child listed.

Your Child's Favorites	
snack	
sport	
author	
restaurant	

Your Favorites	
snack	
sport	
author	
restaurant	

STEP 2 After discussing the choices made in Step 1, have your sixth-grader write sentences identifying his or her favorite things from the chart. Then, have him or her write sentences using your list of favorite things. Your child should vary the wording in each sentence.

> **EXAMPLES** I like strawberries.   Dad's favorite snack is kiwi fruit.
> I love basketball.   My dad prefers tennis.

STEP 3 Tell your child that a semicolon can be used to combine two sentences that are closely related in meaning. Then, have your child combine the related sentences from Step 2.

> **EXAMPLES** I like strawberries; Dad's favorite snack is kiwi fruit.
> I love basketball; my dad prefers tennis.

STEP 4 Your child might want to use this activity as a way to get to know others. He or she could send a chart like the one in Step 1 to relatives or pen pals.

Using Correct Spelling

Dear Parent or Guardian,

Your sixth-grader is currently studying spelling in Chapter 14 of the *Holt Handbook* (California Written and Oral English-Language Conventions Standard 1.5). To give your child extra practice spelling words with *ie* and *ei,* you may wish to use the following information and activity.

Have you ever heard this old rhyme?

RHYME *I* before *e*
Except after *c*
Or when sounded like *a*
As in *neighbor* and *weigh.*

EXAMPLES achieve, belief, receive, ceiling
eight, reindeer

The rules in this rhyme can be helpful reminders when spelling words with *ie* and *ei.* Of course, as with most spelling rules, there are exceptions. If in doubt about a word's spelling, consult a dictionary.

EXCEPTIONS either, neither, leisure, seize, ancient

Rhyme Time

STEP 1 With your child, list several words that rhyme with each of the following words: *achieve, belief, eight, field,* and *weigh.* Try to list as many words as possible that have *ie* or *ei* spellings. Here are some sample words. Can you and your child think of any words to add?

EXAMPLES **achieve:** deceive, relieve
belief: brief, leaf
eight: date, freight
field: chilled, yield
weigh: may, sleigh

STEP 2 Next, help your child write a short poem using the words from the list above. The poem may be serious or funny. Encourage your child to be creative and to have fun.

EXAMPLE After hearing about all we had **achieved,**
I admit I was mighty **relieved**
when the speaker announced his **belief**
that the final speech should be **brief.**

STEP 3 If you and your child enjoyed this activity, you may want to ask him or her to add more lines to the poem or to write a different poem. Your child may also enjoy illustrating the poem.

Using Compound Verbs to Combine Sentences

Dear Parent or Guardian,

   Your child is currently studying Chapter 16 of the *Holt Handbook* to learn how to use compound verbs to combine sentences (California Written and Oral English-Language Conventions Standard 1.1). To provide your child with extra practice combining sentences using compound verbs, you may wish to use the information and the activity provided in this letter.

When the subject (what a sentence is about) of two sentences is the same, you can sometimes combine the two sentences by using a *compound verb*. A **compound verb** is made up of two or more verbs (action or being words) connected by the word *and, or,* or *but*.

> **ORIGINAL** A photographer might work for a newspaper. A photographer might open a portrait studio. [Both sentences have the same subject, *photographer*.]

> **COMPOUND VERB** A photographer **might work** for a newspaper **or might open** a portrait studio. [The verb from each original sentence has been joined with the conjunction *or*.]

Working for a Living

STEP 1 Have your child imagine that he or she is preparing for a career-day presentation at school. Using the chart below, help your child list some careers that he or she might like to pursue someday. Then, work together to jot down two duties that go along with each of these careers. The duties should be described as actions. Here's an example.

Title of Person with Career	Job Duties
Nurse	cares for sick people assists doctors

STEP 2 Next, help your child write a single sentence about each duty listed. Each sentence should begin with the name of the career.

> **EXAMPLE** A nurse cares for sick people. A nurse assists doctors.

STEP 3 Now it's time for your child to combine the two sentences for each career into one sentence that has a compound verb. To help your child use a compound verb, have him or her write one sentence that includes the two duties.

> **ORIGINAL** A nurse cares for sick people. A nurse assists doctors.

> **COMPOUND VERB** A nurse **cares** for sick people **and assists** doctors.

STEP 4 If your child enjoyed talking about careers, he or she may want to do some additional research about a particular career.